THE
RIVER
OF
LIFE
POETRY
COLLECTION

Susan P Doherty

AuthorHouse™ UK
1663 Liberty Drive
Bloomington, IN 47403 USA
www.authorhouse.co.uk
UK TFN: 0800 0148641 (Toll Free inside the UK)
UK Local: 02036 956322 (+44 20 3695 6322 from outside the UK)

The views expressed in this work are solely those of the author and do not necessarily reflect the views of the publisher, and the publisher hereby disclaims any responsibility for them.

This book is printed on acid-free paper.

ISBN: 978-1-7283-7578-6 (sc)
ISBN: 978-1-7283-7577-9 (e)

Library of Congress Control Number: 2022918635

Print information available on the last page.

Published by AuthorHouse 24/10/2022

This book will be registered in the following libraries.
The British Library, Agency for the Legal Deposit Library, Bodleian Libraries of the University of Oxford, Cambridge University Library, The National Library of Scotland, The Library of Trinity College of Dublin, National Library of Wales

authorHOUSE®

Contents

Dedication

I would like to dedicate this book to the memory of my dear friend Michelle Mullin who passed away on 31 May 2021.

You gave me so many memories that I will always treasure

God called and sadly you had to leave

Rest easy with the angels above

And every now and again look down upon us with your never-ending love

About the Book

The River of Life Poetry Collection is a book of thirty poems created over a few years. The poems are not based on any real life situations. However, reflection, observation and imagination, would inevitably have played a part in their formation. The words have not been forced but gently flowed, outlining the beauty and wonder of life, recording precious moments but also noting life's fragility and value. Readers may find that the language used within some of the poems resonates with their own life experiences, therefore, bringing memories to the fore. Each of the poems tells its own creative story for the reader, outlining the natural course of life that can be filled with so much happiness and joy but may also be tinged with immense sadness and pain. The reader will have the opportunity to identify with the stories portrayed, whether this is from the innocence of youth through to older age or sharing their journey with someone special as an adult. A few poems demonstrate the imperfections of people and the devastation caused while others represent kindness and devotion, offering a reminder to the reader of the importance of words and the way in which they are used.

Introduction

The River of Life Poetry Collection takes readers on a journey triggering memories and emotions including feelings of happiness, joy, sadness and grief. From innocent love to deep affection and lifetime commitment as we grow older. Emphasising the value of friendship and support and importance of offering a helping hand. A few poems describe a darker side of human behaviour where much pain and loss is outlined. The poetry reflects the fragility of life, human weakness, heartbreak and the tenderness of new love and eternal love. Describing the gentleness of the heart and the importance of keeping the flame of life alight. The river flowing offers a link to nature as we make so many choices and decisions in life with many unexpected twists and turns as "The words begin to flow". Life is filled with many challenges and these test our limits but we can also derive great strength from them enabling us to continue living. The latter part of the book has a few poems that provide comforting words and offer some hope for recovery and moving forward. Noting that everything in life does not always have a happy ending.

The River of Life

From the moment of birth we enter the flow
An unimaginable journey as off we go
Floating along, gently weaving our way through
Supported and carefully nurtured, everything is so new

As we grow older the river widens, increasing the options
Shaping and forming, sending us in many directions
The currents gradually strengthen, rippling sounds
Encouraging us to make life-changing decisions abound

Sometimes external forces disturb the energy, causing an overflow
Rising waters dimming the light, casting an unwelcome shadow
Dragging us down, slipping beneath, lost in fear
Causing distress, heart stopping panic and despair

Feeling worthless and overwhelmed, trying to keep the mind intact
Frantically swimming, trying to overcome the negative impact
Kindness of a stranger who reaches out their hand, pulling you to safety once more
Heart beats more slowly, calmness and faith in humanity is restored

A Mother's Love

One of life's most precious gifts is a Mother's love
From the first glimpse of their newborn baby's eyes and touch of their soft skin
Nourishing a special bond that was created from within
Softness, gentleness, kindness radiating from their heart

Many Mother's hearts are filled with sadness and pain
Loss of dearest babies and children who had to depart
Sadly not for this time but have left behind a broken heart
Little angels asleep in the arms of God again

A precious giving of their time always putting themselves last
Rarely is a frown or cross word ever cast
A warm smile or precious embrace
Ensuring home is a warm and welcoming space

Always there to listen to our troubles and woes
Crying babies, sleepless nights, terrible twos and tantrums galore
Dealing with stroppy teenagers, banging doors, fits of rage and much more
Falls and breaks and heart stopping moments, every mother knows

Teaching, guiding, baking, sewing, driving us to all our activities and classes
Allowing us freedom to travel on life's journey in our own way
Picking us up when we fall, comforting and putting a plaster on our wounds
Supporting not judging, gently wiping the tears away

Precious memories of Mothers and Grandmothers no longer with us
Generations of love intertwined with the branches of life
Cherish your Mother and hold her close and show her how much she is appreciated
A Mother's love will be there with you for eternity

Gentle Heart

Thump thump echoes the heart as it pulses gently
Sometimes its rhythm is weak, beating slowly, struggling to make its way
Broken heart dealing with tragedy, carrying unbearable pain
Loss of a loved one, life will never seem the same again

Heavy heart weighing deep in our chest
Joy and happiness, miracles of life and sorrows of death, following life's quest
Heart strings stretched and tested beyond their limitations,
Memories of loved ones forever encrypted within

Regularly beating more intensely, rapid and strong
Sharing our heart freely, tenderly ticking along
Heart filled with compassion and endearing love
Reflection of the true kindness and internal beauty gifted from above

Selfish hearts often filled with bad deeds, cold and bleak
Unkind thoughts and cruel actions, an unwelcome clique
Life ripped apart, shredded into tiny pieces, destroying life's beat
Shattering like broken glass, fragmented for eternity

Time doesn't stay with us for long and hearts move on
Pressures and burdens have eased, now just memories of a lifetime gone
The beat of the heart changes and its power is no more
Stillness of heart arrives, never for us to restore

Growing Old

Growing old is the natural way of life and our given destiny
From the crib to our youth the years fly by
Mother Nature nourishes and guides us along
Our chosen journey and life experiences make us strong

Enjoying life and working hard in our career
Cherishing our family and everyone we hold dear
Sharing your life with a special someone
Travelling and seeing the world, having fun

Taking retirement and having a life of leisure
Spending time with family and friends
Grabbing every opportunity and being proud of our achievements
Making fond memories and doing things that give us pleasure

The signs of growing old sneak up on us as time forges ahead
Worrying about our health and if we can remain active become a dread
Unable to do hobbies and activities as our bodies become infirm and weak
Trips and slips due to unsteadiness on our feet

Wrinkles and laugh-lines appear showing life maturity
Getting forgetful or developing dementia and losing respect and dignity
Friends and family passing on, no longer a cherished partner to hold, leaving us isolated
and alone
Needing full-time care and having to leave our home

Growing old is life's process
In our minds we never age, yet the image in the mirror shows confliction
It's the circle of life paving the way for each new generation
Sharing our knowledge and providing them with good direction

Friendship

Friends are beautiful caring people you meet on life's path
Celebrating achievements and having a good laugh
Adding value to your existence, sharing in your dreams
Offering warmth and kindness, raising your confidence and self-esteem

Considerate of feelings providing genuine honesty and affections
Supporting and sharing and non-judging of our imperfections
Never raising an eyebrow or reacting with a frown
Always able to be yourself and they won't ever let you down

A special bond that lasts through the years
Being able to talk about your worries and innermost fears
Enjoying precious moments often getting up to mischief and strife
Filling each day with joy and improving the quality of your life

Patient and understanding being your rock to lean on
Picking you up when you fall and making you strong
Giving generously of their time when in need
Their trust and loyalty will never deplete

Friends can exist on so many levels and in numbers be few
It's how they improve and shape your life that needs to be true
Filling your days with fun and heart-warming pleasure
Good friends are something very special to treasure

In the Light of the Eye

The tool for vision, the gift of sight to be treasured
Offering an insight into the world, wonderful pleasures
Sparkling and shining bright when you see that special one
Instant attraction, new acquaintance or a lifetime companion

Shutters opening and closing, protecting and shielding
Casting their glance, trying not to be too revealing
Forming pictures and images, recording them inside in our mind
Analysing and linking them to opinions and experiences enshrined

Not seeing what is in front of you, not looking deep within
Staring deeply, glaring defiantly, forceful and mean
Startled and filled with fear, as the body is struggling to breathe
Displaying unwelcome emotions hidden beneath

Emotionally charged, as we care for a loved one who is fragile and weak
Weary through ongoing anxiety and prolonged lack of sleep
Smouldering reflection and sultry, filled with love and compassion
Shedding tears for abundant joy or devastating heartache and pain

Capturing scenes of beauty, mountains, landscapes and waterfalls, amazing views
Clearly being able to see and identify family and friends, their images so true
Experiencing the magical birth of babies, renewal of life in nature's way
Filled with great happiness and joy, precious appreciation through the light of the eye.

Valentine's Day

Happy Valentine's Day to all of you
A day when symbols of love may be given
Red roses, soft toys and teddy bears galore
Actions filled with hugs and much more

Memories of love from years of old
Sweet dreams and secrets never to be told
Laughter and childhood romance
Bygone years with holidays and dance

A day often tinged with some blue
As loved ones are no longer here with you
Alone on this day needing compassion and love
Sending their eternal messages of love from above

Relationships having fallen through or gone cold
The wrong time and shattered hopes as dreams unfold
A day dreaded as tears fall from the heart for what may have been
Keeping strong and moving on as the new Horizon remains unseen

A day of hope filled with thoughtfulness and gestures of kindness
In a world that is often full of hatred and harshness
And who knows maybe next time Cupid will send his arrow through
As a special someone may have a sparkle in their eye just for you

Love in a Text

I saw him sitting on the bus just a few seats away, immediately I was drawn to him
Chatting happily and laughing with his friends, looking so handsome
He seems popular with the others I thought, yet he wasn't rough or rowdy
With his dark spiked hair and casual look, he'd be easily noticed in the crowd

I hadn't noticed him before, but had just started a new school a few weeks previously
I guessed he would be a few years older than me as he goes to the local university
I didn't say anything to the other girls as I knew they would just mock me and laugh
Tell me not to waste my time, he's way out of my league, I'd be making a major gaff

As the bus approached our stop, I made my way up the aisle, the bus braked sharply and I stumbled forward losing my balance tumbling downwards, unmistakeable fear taking over
Suddenly everything stopped, time seemed frozen, as a strong hand reached out and grabbed my shoulder
He stepped back to let me pass and greeted me with a warm smile asking if I was ok
Mortified, I thanked him and hoped he couldn't see the heat rising to my face as I hurried away

A few days later I saw him again and this time we were waiting in the bus queue
Just the two of us that particular day, I didn't know where to turn, how to get away
He said hi and told me his name, smiling warmly looking directly at me, his eyes strikingly blue
I told him my name trying to calm my breathing, trying hopelessly to prevent my dreaded blush

As the bus arrived we stepped on board side by side, closely connected yet free
Standing a little behind me, he softly asked if the seat beside me was taken
Heart thumping, his sweet voice causing so many reactions and feelings inside me to awaken
He chatted to me freely and made me feel comfortable, conversation was light and flowed easily

Just as we approached the bus stop he asked if it was ok to share our contact numbers
So he could message as he really enjoyed chatting to me and I happily agreed
Much later that evening I asked myself if I had just been dreaming, was he making a fool, playing a game
And just like that I heard my mobile ping, a smiley with a heart emoji asking if he could see me again

If you could see inside my heart

If you could see inside my heart
The rhythm swiftly fades when we are apart
How it radiates when you are close by
Feeling light and upbeat, soaring so high

Each time that we differ I can feel it weaken
Filled with sorrow, painfully stricken
Harsh words and actions of hatred threaten to tear it
Weighing heavily, overwhelming and crushing my spirit

You fill my life with such happiness and eternal calm
Enfolded within your arms, protecting me from all harm
Knowing I am wanted and cherished, fulfilling my dreams
Sharing in your wonderful moments, my life to redeem

Captivated by You

From the moment of first sight
A vision shining so bright
Totally captivated by you my sweet one
My heart became undone

To be held and to hold
Strong bonds of love unfold
Two souls just where they belong
Growing passionate and strong

Holding hands glancing into each other's eyes
Devoted hearts joined with eternal ties
Cupid loaned me his bow so I could send you my heart
Dressed with so much love never to part

Sharing and nurturing true love's blessing
Loving, caressing with heart filled expressing
Strong sensations and intimate desires
Stirring deep smouldering fires

The smell and softness of your hair
Best friends with so much love and joy to share
The soft touch of your skin, eternal beauty within
The sweet taste of your lips, kisses soft and gentle therein

I love your radiant smile and tender embrace
Beautiful moments, I'm enjoying the chase
Waiting on you to fall into my arms
To protect and support you from life's harms

My Wedding Day

So many years have passed since that first day we met
We were so young, just chilling and having fun, life wasn't serious just yet
Then you enlisted and were dispatched off to do your duty for war
The separation from you off fighting in foreign lands was so hard to bear

Anxiously waiting for your letters, each carefully scribed by your own hand
Describing the beautiful landscapes and surrounding land
Outlining your deep sadness at the destruction of buildings and human life
Telling me as soon as the war would end we would become husband and wife

Then everything fell silent, no letters arrived through my door
The anguish of not knowing if you were alive was so difficult to endure
Your family eventually received a letter to say you were missing, presumed dead
We didn't know you had been captured and harshly imprisoned in a camp instead

I resigned myself to my loss and tried to move on with life
With my heart so heavy and filled with unimaginable grief
Two soul mates experiencing the happiness and innocence of youth
We had enjoyed so many moments of joy and love, your letters as everlasting proof

Five years later a knock on the door presented me with a heart stopping fright
Instantly recognisable grown up man, no longer a youth, a wonderful sight
You had escaped and been recovering with a foreign family, offering fearless kindness
I will be eternally grateful to that family for rescuing you, my respect for them is limitless

You kept your promise from the letters and asked me to be your bride
Before I could accept I had a secret to share which I hoped would fill you with pride
You had become a dad, a little boy created from our selfless love in our earlier youth
The smile on your face as you folded me into your arms was my eternal proof

Months of preparation visiting the bridalwear stores
Choosing the reception venue, band, cake and decorative flowers
Looking for what everyone describes as the perfect dress
Trying to deal with so many challenges and coping with the stress

An exciting and happy day to be treasured and most of all enjoyed
As we receive God's blessing and in matrimony are finally joined
A long awaited time to share our love and happiness with our family
As the music plays softly, my heart beats slowly and happily

The Promise

Walking hand and hand along the beach, my love for my sweetheart grows
Soaking in the sweet smell of the sea and feeling the soft sand between our toes
An air of romance floating along with the summer breeze
Waves crashing, rising and falling, surfers catching them with such ease

Families having picnics and building castles in the sand
Life was wonderful then as our future was planned
Each summer we came to this beautiful, tranquil place
Living the simple life in a rickety camper van, our treasured space

Our families hadn't been happy with our union so at first we had run away
As I proposed to you I promised that we would come back to this place one day
Dancing by the beautiful sunsets and under the dazzling moonlit skies, so happy
Feeling so together, our spirits free, yet joined for all eternity

As the years passed we got married and had two beautiful girls
Twins so much like you with their beautiful brunette curls
Then one morning as you were doing the school run, tragedy struck
A drink driver jumped the lights ploughing straight into you with a huge truck

Our family life changed forever that fateful day
Everything we had taken for granted before had been taken horribly away
When I got the call I rushed to the hospital to hear that the girls were intact
The Emergency services explained your side had taken most of the impact

With severe trauma to your brain and spinal injury, you were in a fractured state
Days of highs and lows, not knowing if each was going to be your last, an excruciating wait
Your injuries were so severe you were no longer able to walk and became confined to a wheelchair
The worthlessness you felt at being unable to do things for yourself was difficult to bear

Battling with infection after infection as they ravaged your weakened frame
The injuries had been so severe many of your organs just couldn't be repaired again
The doctors told me that fluid was building and that unfortunately you were not going to recover
The devastating truth we were going to lose you, my beautiful wife and my babies' mother

I began to make plans with the girls and our reconciled family to take you to our special place
It was a beautiful day and the sun was shining so brightly, the girls said it was just ace
We chatted freely, reliving the memories of those wonderful early days
When we fell so deeply in love, in our more youthful ways

You asked me to always look after the girls to encourage them with their dreams
I made a new promise not to let them forget you and to stay a united family team
I held your hand as your breathing began to change and called the girls close, my heart beating fast
As a family we had our final embrace and our hearts broke as you breathed your last

Life's Trial

As I sit here waiting, wondering what the outcome will be
Situated at the edge of a precipice, pondering what truly is my destiny?
With confusing thoughts and struggling with an array of emotional distress
Weathering the daily furore, growing increasingly restless

Life's burden weighs heavily on my mind
The passage of time seems relentlessly unkind
Lack of understanding and consideration in their words and tasks
Unwillingness to listen, to see or to hear our humble asks

Flame of Life

Flickering and glowing yellow, orange and white
Some people are like flames shining very bright
Humbly supporting and cherishing in their quiet way
A kind word or gesture or gentle touch each day

Flowing and warming and protecting from the cold
Homely at the fireside comforting and relaxing
Celebrating birthdays, weddings and religious occasions
The happiness in eyes as they excitedly wait to blow out candles both young and old

A careless or thoughtless action in an outdoor shared space
A smouldering light very frightening and spreading in the gentle breeze
Fierce and ferocious causing destruction and devastation to people and places
Loss of memories and possessions and links to our past

Showing the way and guiding through darkness and despair
Symbol of faith, solace and prayer
Offering peace and calmness of mind and heart
Human kindness at times of sadness and grief when people are so far apart

Fragile and temporary in its nature
Bringing joy to people in times of worry, pain or need
Easily extinguished by a gentle breath, touch or unkind deed
Precious light to be nurtured as not easily reignited

A Lifetime of Love

A Lifetime filled with such endearing love
Our shared destiny gifted from above
So much happiness and joy as we made our way through life
A loving and devoted husband and wife

The day I proposed I looked into your sparkling blue eyes that glistened with tears
And touched your golden blond hair, that changed so gradually to silver over the years
You made me so happy a life filled with immense joy
We became a beautiful family, blessed with both a girl and a boy

The warmth and beauty of your smile
A truly gentle person always going the extra mile
Always showing others such compassion and care
I don't think I ever saw you frown and if you did it was extremely rare

We met all those years ago on our first day at school
You were very shy and I was running around acting the fool
I knew from that very first glance
It was like finding myself in a trance

As I sit here beside your bed
My mind is in turmoil and filled with despair and dread
It happened so suddenly and made you very ill
The doctors did many tests but there was no cure, no magic pill

I watched you suffer so much pain
You were so calm and never once did you complain
My heart is sore and I'm overcome with absolute grief
As you take your last breath and get your eternal relief

A Youthful Courage

The excitement at signing up, many a young lad's dream
Feeling the bravado with my friends, growing up fast at just sixteen
Wearing the uniform with its khaki array, beaming with pride
Enjoying the attention and glances from the girls as we went on parade

Being able to leave school and travel to lands far from my home
Becoming a soldier, protecting the vulnerable from attackers, still to us unknown
Learning new skills, becoming physically fit, making new friends
Completing the challenges in preparation, as our role in the war transcends

Nervous tension and anticipation is in the training base today
Rumour has it that we are to be shipped before dawn, without delay
A chance to write a letter sending our best thoughts and love to family
Gathering our gear together as an army united, then boarding the truck silently

The journey seemed so long, hours passed as we travelled across rough terrain
No hope of sleep, keeping watch, in a state of constant alertness we must remain
Finally we arrive near a forest and start to dismount, just as the sky turns dark and grey
Immediately we are surrounded by loud bangs and flashes, a barrage of shooting and
bombs come our way

With adrenalin rushing through our veins we run for cover, a planned ambush it would
appear
Panicked and filled with fear, the awful reality of war has now become clear
The sounds around are deafening, ear piercing screams of casualty after casualty as
they fall
There's no bravado now as we lay low, with the dark, wet trenches acting as our
protective wall

I hear shouts of gas! gas! Orders to quickly get our masks in place
A dangerous chemical weapon used by the enemy to deliver death's embrace
As I look around me I see so many bodies lying deathly still
Shattered to pieces, taken so horribly at the pleasure of a tyrant's will

I can't feel my legs, maybe it's just the shock or the cold night air taking hold
There was so much gunfire, just too much for my khaki uniform to withhold
As my mind and broken body are weighed down in agonising pain
I've a strong longing to see my family home once again

Crimson Red

Buildings blown apart, demolished in an instant
No longer recognisable as homes, churches, theatres
Beautiful architecture once enjoyed by so many reduced to dust on the ground
Families separated never to be reunited

So many young lives shattered, sent off to battle for their country
Hoping to come back as heroes, many never to return
No true warning of the actual reality of war for them that lay ahead
The cruelty of war leaving an indelible past

Skies filled with smoke and smells of gunpowder as canons blast throughout the day
Battle cries and shouts of bravado as each battalion forges forward against their enemy
Medical doctors and nurses caring for the wounded, trying to rebuild their broken bodies and traumatised minds
Camps established to hold prisoners treating them badly and with contempt, trying to break their spirits

Children taken from the life they knew, dispatched to other countries
Entering a scary new world, language barriers, cultures so different
Many orphaned, feeling so frightened and alone
No personal belongings, items of comfort from home

Fields filled with the war dead scattered without respect or any human dignity
The soil beneath soaked with their blood now a crimson red
The years have passed by and nature has reclaimed her space
An eerie silence and a deep coldness fills the air at this resting place

Darkness at Christmas

Smiling as I gently place the beautiful crystal bauble on the Christmas tree
Suddenly a harsh voice thunders through the room sending shivers through me
The bauble slips from my trembling hands and crashes to the ground beneath
Fragments of my life shattering everywhere as I struggle to breathe

As I look down with despair in my heart, torn and filled with terror
With a strangely strong desire to turn around and face my tormentor standing there
Dark visions and memories flooding through my mind overwhelmingly
My options are limited, they are so much bigger and stronger than me

I can feel them moving closer and their poisonous scent filling the air potently
Their heavy breathing and clumsy footsteps making their way towards me
My heart beating rapidly and stomach wrenching, what to do, there's nowhere to flee
Suddenly grasped by the back of the head and pulled to the ground violently

Everything has become very still and I am having difficulty trying to see
My head hurts, everything is a blur and my body aches incredibly
Immediately it dawns on me that I am in dark confinement
I call out praying my cries and pleas for help will be heard imminently

Instantly my eyes open widely, I am extremely alert and spring upright
Drenched in perspiration and shivering with relief, what a horrible fright
As I realise this has been a nightmare, a flashback to a former time
A dreadful disturbing childhood memory that resurfaces frequently at Christmastime

Don't be Afraid - Life can get better

Living in the depths of despair
Body bloodied and battered with bruises everywhere
Feeling of worthlessness, abused and controlled
Seems so far away from the words to love and behold

Deep fear and darkness threatens to overcome
Forced separation from family and friends, cut off from everyone
So many promises of hope, love and protection
Have ended in years of violence and ongoing rejection

Relationship has gone so wrong, soured way beyond repair
Broken promises, shattered dreams and inner terror
Enduring torture, physical, emotional and mental pain
Crippling fear of leaving and starting again

Shivering and quivering with overwhelming fear
Feeling so fragile in mind the possibility of a way out isn't clear
Heart beating rapidly struggling to breathe
The children are young so how could you leave

Is there any chance of escaping of getting far away?
It's so tiring living a life in utter desperation and dismay
You said it's my own fault I am totally to blame
How can I let people see what I have become and live with the shame

Is there anyone out there who could come to my aid?
A worthless version of my former self, constantly afraid
Could I be brave and find the courage to make that plea
I really hope one day life can be better for me

Loneliness

Sitting by myself feeling so alone
Isolated and sad, chilled to the bone
No one calls to say hello for a friendly chat
No cards or letters landing on the doormat

You've been gone now for a few years
For you, I have cried so many tears
At the beginning people came but numbers dwindled as time passed
Families leading their busy lives, it couldn't last

Long days fade into longer nights
House holds no warmth or comforting lights
Winter time is the worst when darkness falls
Feeling lost just staring into space or at the walls

Money is less plentiful now but I get the benefits I'm due
It doesn't take much to keep me, my needs are few
I wish you knew how much you are missed, without you my life is so bleak
My heart feels so heavy, worthless and weak

What I would give to hear your voice again
Someone to talk with or listen to, a trusted companion
You filled my life with music and dance which I truly enjoyed
The day you left my life fell silent, a deafening void

As I sit here beside the fireside and the embers burn low
I've a few pieces of coal left for tomorrow
I wonder will it be long before I get my ticket to board Heaven's train
For the angels to take me to be with you again.

Lost

As the lighthouse lights shine bright to guide the boats safely on their way
News has arrived that a number of fishing vessels haven't yet returned today
All our families united in their distress rush to the water's edge
Falling to our knees, praying for the safety of loved ones is our pledge

Waiting, wondering, standing by the harbour walls
My anxiety increasing as the ferocious waves rise and fall
Watching out towards the horizon as far as the eye can see
Hoping yet knowing what the outcome could possibly be

Dreaming and deep felt wishing versus reality
Three hours later the rescue team made their return
Alas only one additional crew on board, a precious freight
Thankfully alive, but in an extremely weakened state

24 hours have now passed and world seems to have stood still
The sea is much calmer now, yet my mind is in absolute turmoil
The rescue boats have been out searching since dawn
Word has filtered through that they are returning, having withdrawn

Their news is bleak as the skipper makes his way towards me
A haunting sound escapes from me, everything turns black
My world collapses as my walls of defence come crashing down
Knowing that my cherished family is lost forever at sea, never coming back

The whole village is in mourning a terrible sadness all around
Their kindness and support shows no bounds
As they try to make sense of this devastating tragedy
The fishermen families constantly aware of the risks, the potential for catastrophe

As my teardrops fall softly on the ground, flowing unrestrained
Their stain spreading out widely becoming deeply ingrained
The loss of my husband and two teenage sons feeling broken, never to recover
My life is so empty with no purpose, no bodies ever discovered

I don't know how much longer I can go on, my never-ending plight
I walk to the shoreline every morning and night
So many thoughts of what may have been, our future we had planned side by side
Asking God why? Begging for release from my torment, to let this pain subside

Kindness

Be kind each and every day
To all you spend time with at home, in work and at play
Don't get caught up in social media frenzy or office chatter
Stay clear of the cruelty that makes lives shatter

Thinking before you speak and if there's nothing nice just refrain
Words can cause so much anxiousness and pain
Not casting judgement or passing unfair comment
Do not utter words of disdain or unwarranted intent

A kind gesture such as giving up your seat
A thoughtful word or helping hand while remaining discreet
Letting someone ahead of you in a queue
Sure what's the rush it's only an extra minute or two

You don't know the worries that others carry in their heart
To protect the vulnerable each of us must play our part
Stresses weighing heavily on their mind
How hard is it to become less selfish and kind?

Healing Hands

The gift of healing hands so gentle and strong
Applying their soft touch, light pressure gliding along
Skilled instruments guided by signals from the brain
Artistic in their movements, knowledgeable in their domain

Lifting and holding, caring for the incapacitated and weak
Promoting healing, restoring their external physique
Comforting, supporting, easing their inner pain
Freeing them from their burden, bearing the strain

Understanding, reaching out, relieving accumulated stress
Mending the hurts, repairing the fractures of life's emotional distress
Steadying, reinvigorating through kindness and dedicated care
Strengthening and improving quality of life through the gift they share

It's been a While

It's been a while since I saw your kind and happy face
Our lives were turned upside down, sending us to a dreadful place
I've missed your smile and hearing your soft voice
You were taken so suddenly, we had no choice

When we lost you time seemed to stand still
But the world moved on, a strange but bitter pill
When you left our hearts were filled with pain, truly broke
We didn't know how we were going to manage, be able to cope

Sharing our stories as we walked along side by side
Admiring nature's beauty and listening to sounds of the countryside
The last 12 months have passed by so fast
My memories of our time together will forever last

Each morning we are fortunate to experience a new dawn
We make the effort to go about our daily lives trying to be strong
Our hearts will always hold a heaviness we cannot undo
A deep void and sadness as we no longer have you

We know that God needed someone to help with his tasks
He gave you your heavenly wings, someone special he could ask
As each day begins we hold our head up high
As we know you will always be close by

Forgiveness for Me

The wound is raw, deep and weeping, never healing
Permanent scarring as a painful reminder of my unimaginable shame
Memories of mistreatment of the worst kind, delivered with intent
Displays of nastiness and hatred, cruel behaviour and action

Feeling weak and insecure, shivering, lying on the cold, damp floor
Letting the overwhelming feelings go, tears way past the brim of overflow
Trying to see through the dark agonising pain, everything is like a fog
Heart weighed down, crushed through the years, as dreams fell apart

Controlled and hidden, separated from family and friends, relentless isolation
Misplaced loyalty, obedient, pleasant and consistently amenable
Tricked and charmed, pretentious promises of a wonderful life
Trusting and naïve, so generous to share my kindness and love

Having escaped that lifetime, no longer part of a narcissist's twisted game
Moving forward, a determined desire to feel whole and well again
Lifting a heaviness from my heart, not holding on to mind-weary grudges
Setting free, forgiving but remembering, separating the perpetrator from me

Tipping the Scales

Weighing up your options, making personal choices
Often following others, taking on board external voices
Fearing the worst, tiptoeing steadily along
Feelings of guilt or failure, worrying about getting things wrong

Trembling at the knees, always trying to please
Bound by life's chains, constantly ill at ease
Trying to do the right thing, abiding by the rules
Reality versus dreaming, life can seem cruel

Feeling overwhelmed while juggling everyday tasks
Knowing when things become too much, taking off your mask
Releasing your inner self-esteem, holding your nerve
True grit and determination, will get the results you deserve

Letting go

People display many types of personality and behavioural traits
Some are kind, loving and generous with their time
Others are like predators, charming at first but in reality playing with your mind
Drawing their victims in through a web of false promises and lies

The cloak surrounding you weighs heavily upon your tiny frame
Wrapped tightly around you for so many years
It has been absorbing all the trauma that has been sent your way
Acting as your shield as you hid beneath its dark shadow

Not letting others see your physical and mental pain
Struggling to continue carrying your burden
Frightened to take that first step forward, to begin again
Letting go of the hurt, trauma and immense pain

You are not to blame for any of this, you fell in love
Trusted them, believed their every word to be true
Don't be afraid to tell your story, close friends and family will understand
There are many people who will support you and take your hand

Gradually undo each button, slowly releasing their hold on you
Freeing yourself from the harrowing past
You have been so strong, with brave determination
There is a future preparing for you to shine your light again

A Glimmer of Hope

As I sit here alone, staring out the window wondering where it all went wrong
I had so much in my life, a beautiful wife and children and now it's all gone
Life was good, I was filled with determination and drive
I was super confident, you could say exuding with pride

Extremely successful at my job having been promoted several times
The money was plentiful, my status was prime
Playing football with my colleagues twice a week and training at the gym
In my mind I was invincible, not realising my capacity was almost at the brim

We started to visit a local bar just for the one, the others encouraged me, and I wanted to fit in
It really did feel good to relax and unwind after each game
At first it was ok and I was able to manage the pace
Then a few months passed and it seemed I never left the place

I was in no hurry home, sure all was well with my family and our fantastic home
How would I have known, I never had the courtesy to check by picking up the phone
My wife started to mention how much I had changed and asked why I was always home late
I was finding it harder to get up each morning, always rushing, getting to work in a dishevelled state

Work was increasing and deadlines seemed to be shorter than they had been previously
The pressure was strong, my work was slipping, and delivery was often with significant delay
Spending so much time in the pub, almost every day, forgetting about the bills I had to pay
The warnings were there but I brushed them away

Red reminder letters arrived and were ignored
I didn't see my wife's sadness and desperation as she begged and implored
The day of reckoning finally came and from my job I was sacked
Who could deny I no longer was effective, the foundations had cracked

Our house was re-possessed and my wife could take no more and taking the children she left
I'm so ashamed now six months later, feeling totally bereft
It took me this long to realise that I had lost all my self-respect and dignity
My overconfident mannerisms and attitude have disappeared completely

The kind stranger who picked me up from the street, giving me shelter, warmth and protection
With food in my stomach and a roof over my head, I no longer feel such bitter rejection
I'm having counselling to deal with my alcohol addiction, trying to make a new start
I deserve my self-inflicted punishment for tearing so many lives apart

There is an old saying that pride often goes before a fall
I sure went to the bottom, but I am determined to climb back up to face it all
I sit here now and wonder about what my future, if any, may bring
Will my family ever be able to forgive me for my failing?

I have written them a letter outlining my deep regret, for their recognition I can only pray and hope
Even just a glimmer would help me to want to go on living and finally be able to cope
To see and speak to my wife and children, those who in my heart I hold dear
I know that I will face a daily battle and from the demon drink must always stay clear

Hold My Hand

Hold my hand
It's time to get up and stand
I can feel your pain
Trust in me, life will begin again

To lose someone so special in your life
A grandparent, parent, child, partner, husband or wife
Their flame of life is no more
Bringing a terrible darkness to your door

So many tears have fallen
Glistening like raindrops on leaves in autumn
The emptiness in your heart
The brokenness of being so far apart

Don't give up, I know words don't seem enough
It was so fortunate to have had their love
They are with the angels heaven sent that fateful day
Don't despair their love will never be far away

You miss their smile, voice and their touch
Most days the overwhelming void just seems too much
Know that you are not alone
Life does go on and you are strong

Cherish the memories and precious times storing them close to your heart
Let them settle within and give you peace of mind letting life restart
Know that time moves swiftly by
One day soon you too will get your angel wings to fly

Words

Words gifted to us from the moment we learn to speak
Enabling us to read books and write our own pieces individual and unique
Encouraged by our parents and teachers each day exploring all the different kinds
Taught and repeated regularly over and over and safely stored in our minds

Formed and shaped in our brain and articulated through our voices
Opening up so many educational opportunities and expanding our choices
Lovingly shared with close family and friends, always being polite
Sadly some people use words that are cruel and filled with hatred and spite

Threatening and forceful and sharp like blades cutting through flesh
Incised wounds deeply ingrained often unable to heal, remaining fresh
Words should be spoken gently and with kindness, considering others feelings
Expressing warmth and welcome through our daily greetings

Acknowledgements

There are so many people who have supported me with the creation of the River of Life Poetry Collection. Firstly, heartfelt thanks to my mum and dad and brothers and sisters who always offer their support and inspire me with the confidence to follow my dreams. My lifelong friends Margaret, Sheila and Theresa who deserve a special mention as they have been my sounding board for so many poems over the last few years offering their honest advice and comments even if that was quite often very late at night. They have provided me with the inspiration to keep writing and to share the poetry with you the reader. I would like to thank Author House and their team for their continuous support and professionalism in enabling me to get my first poetry collection to final publication, fulfilling a long awaited goal.

About the Author

Susan lives in rural County Tyrone, Northern Ireland and it is through her love for walking that she has developed a strong affiliation for the beauty of the countryside. Admiring how nature is interlinked so much with our everyday life and has an appreciation of each sunrise that she gets to experience. Susan is a graduate of Ulster University having gained a BA (Hons) in Business Studies and also a Masters in Business Administration (MBA) and has worked in local government for over 25 years, working both with local businesses and the community and voluntary sector. Over the last few years Susan has rekindled her love for writing poetry and this is her first poetry collection.